Ghetto Love
Part 3
My version
Of
Psalms

I0190246

Sedelia Gardner

Avid Readers Publishing Group

Lakewood, California

Ghetto Love Part 3

My Version of Psalms

Avid Readers Publishing Group

http://www.avidreaderspg.com

ISBN-13: 978-1-61286-152-4

Printed in the United States

The meaning of Ghetto –

1- *It means someone has no class or is very loud and obnoxious.*

2- *If it's a racial situation, it could also be used to describe a black person.*

3- *A ghetto can be a place where poor people live the slums of the city*

4- *If it is the latter, the person is probably finding cheap ways to do things.*

The meaning of Love –

1- *Love is a feeling that really can't be described.*

2- *It's something you can only feel.*

3- *It's about caring for someone deeply, and never wanting to let go.*

4- *It's about thinking about them constantly.*

5- *And no matter what they do, you can never stopping loving them.*

We are all seeds in His precious garden

Some are meant to be planted

Some are meant to be watered

And some are meant for growth

And even thou

He tries to nourish them all

Some still don't make it!

NAMES FOR GOD

- **ELOHIM......Genesis 1:1, Psalm 19:1**

- **meaning "God", a reference to God's power and might.**

- **ADONAI......Malachi 1:6**

- **meaning "Lord", a reference to the Lordship of God.**

- **JEHOVAH--YAHWEH.....Genesis 2:4**

- **a reference to God's divine salvation.**

- **JEHOVAH-MACCADDESHEM.......Exodus 31:13**

- **meaning "The Lord thy sanctifier"**

- **JEHOVAH-ROHI......Psalm 23:1**

- **meaning "The Lord my shepherd"**

- **JEHOVAH-SHAMMAH.......Ezekiel 48:35**

- **meaning "The Lord who is present"**

- **JEHOVAH-RAPHA.........Exodus 15:26**

- **meaning "The Lord our healer"**

- **JEHOVAH-TSIDKENU......Jeremiah 23:6**

- **meaning "The Lord our righteousness"**

- **JEHOVAH-JIREH.........Genesis 22:13-14**

- **meaning "The Lord will provide"**

- **JEHOVAH-NISSI**.........Exodus 17:15

- meaning "The Lord our banner"

- **JEHOVAH-SHALOM**........Judges 6:24

- meaning "The Lord is peace"

- **JEHOVAH-SABBAOTH**......Isaiah 6:1-3

- meaning "The Lord of Hosts"

- **JEHOVAH-GMOLAH**........Jeremiah 51:6

- meaning "The God of Recompense"

- **EL-ELYON**..............Genesis 14:17-20,Isaiah 14:13-14

- meaning "The most high God

- **EL-ROI**................Genesis 16:13

- meaning "The strong one who sees"

- **EL-SHADDAI**............Genesis 17:1,Psalm 91:1

- meaning "The God of the mountains or God Almighty"

- **EL-OLAM**...............Isaiah 40:28-31

- meaning "The everlasting God"

MORE NAMES FOR GOD

- **AVENGER**.........................1Thess.4:6

- **ABBA**.............................Romans 8:15

- **ADVOCATE**............................I John 2:1 (kjv)

- **ALMIGHTY**..........................Genesis 17:1

- **ALL IN ALL**........................Colossians 3:11

- **ALPHA**..............................Revelation 22:13

- **AMEN**..............................Revelation 3:14

- **ANCIENT OF DAYS**..................Daniel 7:9

- **ANOINTED ONE**.....................Psalm 2:2

- **APOSTLE**...........................Hebrews 3:1

- **ARM OF THE LORD**..................Isaiah 53:1

- **AUTHOR OF ETERNAL SALVATION**......
  Hebrews 5:9

- **AUTHOR OF OUR FAITH**..............
  Hebrews 12:2

- **AUTHOR OF PEACE**..................1 Cor.
  14:33

- **BEGINNING**.........................Revelation 21:6

- **BISHOP OF SOULS**...................1 Peter 2:25

- **BLESSED & HOLY RULER**..............1
  Timothy 6:15

- **BRANCH**............................Jeremiah 33:15

- **BREAD OF GOD**......................John 6:33

- **BREAD OF LIFE**.....................John 6:35

- **HEAD OF THE BODY**...................... Colossians 1:18

- **HEAD OF THE CHURCH**...................... Ephesians 5:23

- **HEIR OF ALL THINGS**...................... Hebrews 1:2

- **HIDING PLACE**............................Psalm 32:7

- **HIGHEST**................................Luke 1:76

- **HIGH PRIEST**............................Hebrews 3:1

- **HIGH PRIEST FOREVER**.................... Hebrews 6:20

- **HOLY GHOST**............................John 14:26

- **HOLY ONE**................................Acts 2:27

- **HOLY ONE OF ISRAEL**......................Isaiah 49:7

- **HOLY SPIRIT**............................John 15:26

- **HOPE**....................................Titus 2:13

- **HORN OF SALVATION**......................Luke 1:69

- **HUSBAND**................................Isaiah 54:5,Jere.31:32,Hosea 2:16

- **I AM**....................................Exodus 3:14, John 8:58

- **IMAGE OF GOD**............................2 Cor. 4:4

- IMAGE OF HIS PERSON...................... Hebrews 1:3 (kjv)

- IMMANUEL.................................Isaiah 7:14

- INTERCESSOR.............................Romans 8:26,27,34 Hebrews 7:25

- JAH...................................Psalm 68:4(kjv)

- JEALOUS..............................Exodus 34:14(kjv)

- JEHOVAH.............................Psalm 83:18(kjv)

- JESUS................................Matthew 1:21

- JESUS CHRIST OUR LORD................ Romans 6:23

- JUDGE................................Isaiah 33:22, Acts 10:42

- JUST ONE.............................Acts 22:14

- KEEPER..............................Psalm 121:5

- KING.................................Zechariah 9:9

- KING ETERNAL.........................1 Timothy 1:17

- KING OF GLORY........................Psalm 24:10

- KING OF JEWS.........................Matthew 27:11

- LORD OF ALL...........................Acts 10:36

- LORD OF GLORY ....1 Cor. 2:8

- LORD OF HARVEST.......................
  Matthew 9:38

- LORD OF HOSTS..........................Haggai 1:5

- LORD OF LORDS..........................1 Tim.
  6:15

- LORD OUR RIGHTEOUSNESS..............
  Jeremiah 23:6

- LOVE.................................1 John 4:8

- LOVINGKINDNESS.......................Psalm
  144:2

- MAKER...................................Job 35:10,
  Psalm 95:6

- MAJESTY ON HIGH.......................
  Hebrews 1:3

- MAN OF SORROWS.........................Isaiah
  53:3

- MASTER.................................Luke 5:5

- MEDIATOR...............................1 Timothy
  2:5

- MERCIFUL GOD...........................Jeremiah
  3:12

- MESSENGER OF THE
  COVENANT................Malachi 3:1

- **PRINCE OF LIFE**............................Acts 3:15

- **PRINCE OF PEACE**.........................Isaiah 9:6

- **PROPHET**...................................Acts 3:22

- **PROPHET OF THE HIGHEST**...................
  Luke 1:76

- **PROPITIATION**.............................1John 2:2, 1John 4:10

- **PURIFIER**..................................Malachi 3:3

- **QUICKENING SPIRIT**........................1 Corinthians 15:45(kjv)

- **RABBONI (TEACHER)**.........................John 20:16

- **RADIANCE OF GOD'S GLORY**.................
  Heb.1:3

- **REDEEMER**.................................Job 19:25

- **REFINER'S FIRE**...........................Malachi 3:2

- **REFUGE**...................................Jeremiah 16:19

- **RESURRECTION**.............................John 11:25

- **REWARDER**.................................Hebrews 11:6

- **RIGHTEOUS ONE**........................1 John 2:1

- ROCK..1 Cor.10:4

- ROOT OF DAVID............................Rev. 22:16

- ROSE OF SHARON............................Song 2:1

- RULER OF GOD'S CREATION.................. Rev. 3:14

- RULER OVER KINGS OF EARTH................Rev 1:5

- RULER OVER ISRAEL........................ Micah 5:2

- SAVIOR....................................Luke 2:11

- SCEPTRE...................................Numbers 24:17

- SEED......................................Genesis 3:15

- SERVANT...................................Isaiah 42:1

- SHADE.....................................Psalm 121:5

- SHEPHERD OF OUR SOULS....................1Peter 2:25

- SHIELD....................................Genesis 15:1

- SHILOH....................................Genesis 49:10

- SONG......................................Exodus 15:2, Isaiah 12:2

- SON OF DAVID...........................Matthew 1:1

There are many names for God, and different names are attached to different cultural ideas and beliefs about who God is and what His aspects are. Some do not believe in God at all. I guess they made their steps through life with some sort of invisible energy force. Regardless if you believe in God or the invisible energy something or someone got you through hard times. Something or someone gave you joy in times of sadness. And at least once in your life you had to cry out to God for help. I am sure you were grateful He helped you make it through.

Sedelia Gardner

I refuse to let the residue of others or my past, restrict me from receiving my future results so I brush off my shoulders and continue to praise You!

This book is dedicated to God who has pulled me out of a many of pits! And to my Natural Born Husslers Sheri Coleman, Jessica Perez, Sharon Poole, and Calinda Lucas, Al-Shariyfa Robinson, Angelita Aguilar, Karen Williams and in loving memory of Charlotte Terrell enjoy!

Proverbs 24 3:4 By wisdom a house is built, and through understanding it is established; through knowledge its rooms are filled with rare and beautiful treasures.

HOW I SEE GOD

I see your presence like misty rain

Soft barely seen

But the moisture you leave behind

Lets me know You are there

I hear your voice like birds chirping

Sweet medleys

But even thou I don't understand the song they sing

You place it in my heart to understand the meaning

I feel your touch it's like cotton

Soft barely felt

But the feeling it leaves behind

Let me know You are there

I look to you and I see a light

Shining bright

But even thou I am not worthy the light shine on me still

You placed it in my heart to understand the meaning

Sedelia Gardner

Grateful

You fill me with hope

When I had no hope left

You held my hand

Even when I let yours go

I'm so grateful to have a Father like you

You filled me with love

When I had no love left

You stood by my side

Even when my faith slipped away

I'm so grateful to have a Father like you

You wiped my tears from my eyes

The ones that only you could see

You heard my cries

And I didn't even have to scream

I'm so grateful to have a Father like you

You sacrificed your son for me

So that I may live

And even thou I still sinned

You still continued to bless me

I'm so grateful to have a Father like you

Sedelia Gardner

I was made not to break

The water drips from my eyes
And are quickly absorb into my skin
The tears moisten my skin but it doesn't soften
Because I was made not to break

I was made in your image so
I know I was made not break
So I look to You

The shell of my body receives many blows
From my enemies
But my soul still remains untouched
Because I was made not to break

I am showered with you blessing so
I know I was made not break
So I look to You

The words from my enemies get thrown at me
From all angles and shake me but
My mind is at ease
Because I was made not to break

I am protected by your mercy so
I know I was made not break
So I look to You

Sedelia Gardner

Fly

I finally made it out of my cocoon
And I am doing all that I can
To spread my wings so that I
Can fly

I stumble and I fall
And sometimes my wings aren't strong enough
To hold me up but I still reach for
The sky

I am to strong and I am not weak
I maybe stubborn
But I refuse to sit down and die
When there is a small chance I
Can fly

I spread open my wings
And I spread them open with all my strength
I let go of the bondage that held me down
And I let the sweet winds of mercy carry me to
The sky

Sedelia Gardner

I'll Pray

I can't cry anymore so instead I'll just sit here and pray

I sit all alone in this dark room no one around

But I can feel His presence all around me

I can't cry anymore so instead I'll just here sit and pray

I can't even gather the strength to fuss and fight anymore

My shoulders are weighed down and I'm tired but

I can't cry anymore so instead I'll just sit here and pray

I look all around trying to figure out how this trouble entered my life

My heart is heavy and the pain is taking hold of me but

I can't cry anymore so instead I'll just sit here and pray

The screams won't come out no matter how hard I try

I try to cry but the tears refuse to fall

I can't cry anymore so instead I'll just sit here and pray

Sedelia Gardner

Your Blood Still Works

Through the dark and cloudy storms I stood alone

With my hands stretching out to You

And with you in my heart and I prayed

Through your precious blood I am saved

Because your blood still works

For those that believe

Darker than night itself and deeper than the see I sat alone

And I reached out for You as I cried

And with You in my heart I prayed

Through your precious blood I am saved

Because your blood still works

For those that believe

I prayed to You and the sun came out after the storm

And the sea I was drowning in was now a puddle beneath my feet

And I rejoiced with You in my heart and I sang

Through your precious blood I am saved

Because your blood still works

For those that believe

Sedelia Gardner

Your Hand

I wish I could see Your hand in mine

As we travel together down the road

With Your hand wrapped in mine

I wish I could feel Your hand in mine

As I slip but quickly I am lifted up

As we travel together down the road

With Your hand wrapped in mine

I wanted to see your hand in mine

The one that gives me strength

As we travel together down the road

With Your hand wrapped in mine

I wanted to feel Your hand in mine

But Your presence in the midst alone is good enough

As we travel together down the road

With Your hand wrapped in mine

Sedelia Gardner

Kneel to You

I stood before my enemies

With a back bone that refuse to break

And knees that refused to buckle

Lash after Lash my enemies put upon me

But still I stood

How could I even stand against them

When I have no one standing with me

I stood alone

And I refuse to be broken

Lash after Lash my enemies put upon me

My heart gave in

And my soul cried out

And I went on bended knees

I had to kneel before You first

So I could stop standing alone

I stand now with a back bone

That cannot be broken by man

And knees that only bend for my Father

The whip wraps around my body

But lashes I no longer feel

I had to kneel before You first

Before I could even stand at all

Sedelia Gardner

Shelter Me

Can You come and shelter me

From the storm

If just for a little while

I know there were times when I didn't come to You

And I know there were times when I didn't call out to You

But today my burdens are more than I can bare

Lord you said You will never leave me

So I know You are there

So I ask

Can You come and shelter me

From the storm

If just for a little while

The tears keep falling and I feel my soul getting weak

No one is left in my corner but You

So now we finally speak

Here I am Lord I give it all to You

I tried it on my own

But I can't take another step without You

So I humble myself and ask

Can You come and shelter me

From the storm

If just for a little while

Sedelia Gardner

The Bridge

As

I see the other side

How bright the sun shines

As it rays dance around the green pastures

Just a finger tip away

How will I get there I wondered

As

I sit on the other side

How dark are the clouds around me

As the rain pour down on me

As I look at the sun just a finger tip away

How will I get there I wondered

As

I walk towards the other side

How a bridge was forming beneath my feet with your WORD

As the bridge kept forming the sun was closer than just a finger tip away

How did I get here I wondered

As

I danced on the bridge

How far away the clouds are from me

As the sun shined down on me

I danced around in the green pastures

I looked down and rejoice as I seen the bridge You had made for me

Sedelia Gardner

This Cup

I sip this wine from this cup

In remembrance of You

I break bread with my sisters

Giving thanks for all that You do

You saved me

You saved my soul

And You washed away my sin with your blood

A thing You didn't have to do for me

And when my body

Has withered and gone

This soul that You saved

Will be standing next to You

So I sip this wine from my cup

And I break bread with my sisters

In remembrance of You

Sedelia Gardner

I Sing

I know I sing off key

And to many my voice doesn't sound right

But thinking of all that You have done

Gives me the courage to sing to You

I know I forget some words

And I start to hymn instead

But You knowing the melody of my heart

Gives me the courage to sing to You

I know I am not perfect

And to many I am not right

But thinking of how You love me

Gives me the courage to sing to You

Sedelia Gardner

Take My Hand

Come take my hand

Pull me out of this fire I am in

Let the ground be beneath my feet

So that I can dance in the rays of the sun

Giving thanks to You

Come take my hand

Pull me out of this fire I am in

Lift me high above the ground

So that I can rejoice in clouds up above

Giving my voice to You to sing praises in your name

Come take my hand

Pull me out of this fire I am in

Let the smoke be cleared from the sky

So my eyes can shine once again

Giving the glory to You as I look up above

Lord come and take my hand

Sedelia Gardner

Locust

I stood outside the gates of my garden
And I watched the locust
As they ate their fill of my fruit
I felt I had no defense against the locust
As they ate from my garden

Season after season after season
When will the season of the locust end
When will my garden gain the strength to grow

I stood outside the gates of my garden
And I watched the locust
As the sun shone down upon my fruit
I felt I had gained my defense against the locust
As they ate from my garden

Season after season after season
When the rain came the season of the locust came to an
end
When the sun came out my garden gain the strength to
grow

I stood inside the gates of my garden
And I watched the death of the locust
As I ate my fill of my fruit
I felt I could always win against the locust
As I ate from my garden

Season after season after season
When the sun shined down bringing the season of the
locust to an end
When my garden gain strength each day to grow
I stood inside the gates of my garden
Season after season after season

Sedelia Gardner

Crown Of Thorns

When You came into this world

They gave You silver and gold

But when You left this world for us

They gave You a crown of thorns

They did not know what it was they had done

Just like You washed my sins away

You were washing away their sins as well

My King my precious King

Adorned with a crown of thorns

As they wrapped the branches tightly together

And the thorns pierced your precious head

It started the shed of your precious blood

That now covers and protects me now

My King my precious King

Adorned with a crown of thorns

As I kneel before this thorn bush

I think of how You died so that I may live

No King has ever given his life so that others could live

You saved past and future generations

And they gave You a crown of thorns

Sedelia Gardner

My Eyes

My eyes are to weary

And they cannot see pass the clouds

And even thou I feel the rays of the sun

My eyes are to weary to see it

My eyes are to weary

And they cannot see the moon in the sky

And even thou I know it is there

My eyes are to weary to see it

And they cannot see the green grass up ahead

And even thou I know I no longer walk on rocks

My eyes are to weary to see it

My eyes are to weary

And my God can see farther than me

And even thou I cannot see Him

My weary legs carry me on up ahead

My eyes are to weary

And I don't need them to know He is there

Sedelia Gardner

I Cry Tonight

I will cry tonight

But I will smile with the morning sun

Here I lay in the darkness

Protected by the ever burning light

The light burns brighter as the night goes on

And the darkness of my mind is almost gone

I gave it all to Him

So my work is done

I will cry tonight

But I will smile with the morning sun

Sedelia Gardner

Closed Mouth

I stood there day after day

And even thou the light shined on me

The darkness kept my mouth closed

But the light kept shining down on me

And the darkness slowly lost its hold

My Spirit broke through

And released the words that needed to be heard

My words floated up to heaven

And my blessing poured down on me like a much needed rain

My spirit was now free and my mouth is forever open

And my prayers and praises will be forever heard

As I rejoice in my blessings

Being poured down on me like a much needed rain

Sedelia Gardner

Can't Please Them All

I can make this one smile

And I can make this one cry

I can make this one happy

And I can make this one sad

I can make this one think

And I can make this one mad

I can make this one yell and scream

And I can make this one rejoice and sing

I try to please them all

But I am not getting no were at all

Jesus turned water to wine and some smiled

Jesus healed the sick and gave sight to the blind and some cried

Jesus made the dead rise again and the lame walk and some were happy

Jesus told the truth to many and some were sad

Jesus taught the word to many and this made some think

Jesus cleared out the synagogue and some were mad

Jesus said he was the Son of God and this made some yell and scream

Jesus said He will die and rise again and this made some rejoice and sing

Jesus couldn't please them all

But he still died on the cross for us all

Sedelia Gardner

Don't Have To Beg

I don't have to beg

When I have a Father

That has it all

Even thou my pockets are empty

He said if I ask I shall receive

Health there isn't an aliment He can't cure

Money He has more than my pockets can hold

Relief He can take away the pain

Joy He gave me the Holy Ghost

Lost He will give you guidance

Confused He will work it out

Love He gave us His Son

Protection He will fight your battles

Death He gave us everlasting life

I don't have to beg

When I have a Father

That has it all

Sedelia Gardner

My Climb

I started this journey up this mountain

Hoping that one day I will reach the top

No rope to hold me up

When the rocks crumbled beneath my feet

No shelter to protect me

When the rocks fell down on me

I started this journey up this mountain

Hoping that one day I will reach the top

No rope to pull me up

When the rocks crumbled and dragged me down

No shelter to run to

When the rocks fell and pushed me back

I started this journey up this mountain

Hoping that one day I will reach the top

With hope to hold me up

When the rocks crumbled beneath my feet

With faith to protect me

When the rocks fell down on me

I started this journey up this mountain

Hoping that one day I will reach the top

Sedelia Gardner

Awake

I am wide awake

My Spirit has just been awoken

And my eyes adjust

To the closed doors that are now open

I see the hills that He pushed me over

My eyes adjust

To the mountains that He moved for me

I see how He held me up as I stood

In the waters sinking

I am wide awake

My spirit has just been awoken

Sedelia Gardner

Chalice

Many searched for your chalice to gain a power

They already have the hem of your garment

Gave healing the touch of your hand

Restored sight your spoken words

Rose the dead the shed of your

Blood gave everlasting life

And my faith in you has

Eased my suffering

Why go search

For a chalice

When I all

Ready

Have

The

POWER INSIDE

Sedelia Gardner

Cross Roads

How many times have I stood at the cross roads

How many times did He die on the Cross

Trying to pick from right and wrong at the cross roads

He made one choice and that was the Cross

It is a constant battle at the cross roads

He won my battle for me on the Cross

*One road green one road rocky that is my choice at the
cross roads*

He chose the rocky road that ended with the Cross

Ask him for strength when you stand at the cross roads

Sedelia Gardner

The Breeze

I knelt down in front of the weeping willow tree

To say my prayers and to get an answer

The long hanging branches reminded me of how tired I was

The troubles in my life had weighed me down

I prayed for relief

I prayed for an answer

I shouted for a changed

And I screamed for Him to answer me

With each rant I gave out

A gentle breeze came across the tree

Gently lifting up the hanging branches of the tree

So that they may reach for the heavens if only for a little while

I wanted that strength that the breeze gave to the tree

So I knelt down in front of the weeping willow tree

And I let His breeze come and guide me in a new direction

Sedelia Gardner

Closer to You

Everyone is gone they have all scattered to the ends of the earth

There is no one left by my side but You

Before I am dead and gone

I will take this little bit of faith I have left

And use it to get closer to You

I should have tithed more

Lord I'm sorry

I should have been happy with the small blessing

Lord I'm sorry

I should have helped those in need

Lord I'm sorry

I should have came to You more

Lord I'm sorry

I should have praised You instead of complaining

Lord I'm sorry

I should have kept my faith in You

Lord I'm sorry

I am sorry for all the wrong that I have done

But before I am dead and gone

I will take this little bit of faith I have left

And use it to get closer to You

Sedelia Gardner

Move On

My past is not bright

It is filled with dark moments

Some that only me and God know about

But He let me rise again to see His smile in the sky

So I move on

My choices were not always right

Some filled my life with hell moments

Some choices that only me and God know about

Be He let me fall only to pick me up so my eyes could see His smile in the sky

So I move on

My God is always right

He is with me during every moment

Some that only me and Him know about

But as long as He continue to let me see His smile in the sky

I will move on

Sedelia Gardner

Horizon

My eyes cannot see over the horizon

But still I move closer to it

I am only capable of seeing the rising and sitting of His sun

Will I fall off into the darkness when I reach the horizon

I wonder as I move forward without fear

Sedelia Gardner

History

I drug myself across the rocky road

To climb myself out of my history

I pulled away from the vines behind me

It was my history holding me back

I pushed inch by inch

Crawling over rocks and pulling myself out of pits

To break hold of my history

Finally I have reached solid ground

Green pastures and blue skies

A sigh of relief as the bond is broken

Between me and my history

And my arms stretch forward

To embrace the destiny

You have waiting up ahead for me

Without my history

Sedelia Gardner

Final Say

Some think I am not worthy

Of the blessing that are waiting on me

In the store house waiting to be released

But my Father has the final say

I overcame my trials

And I won the battles with temptation

My reward for the victory is just

My Father has the final say

Some tired to block me from my blessings

A reward based on my faith and the battles won

It is something I am destined to receive

Regardless of the road I take

Their words mean nothing to me

My Father has the final say

Sedelia Gardner

Howl to the moon

There once was a wolf

And his long time pack had left him

Alone, lost and hungry

As he walked across the hot dessert sands

The night swept over the land

Causing everything to disappear in the darkness

Except him

The light of the moon shined down on him

As he laid there dying

He gathered his last bit of strength

To let out one last howl to the light of the moon

His Creator heard his cries

And the stars began to fall down from the skies

And as they landed in front of the dying wolf

A bird appeared for his hunger

A puddle of water for his thirst

And a road appeared in front of him for his travel

The wolf then knew he was longer alone

He had been saved from an early death

He traveled down the new path his Creator had gave to him

And he howled to his Creator in the light of the moon

Sedelia Gardner

Paradise

I am going to paradise

My burdens cannot follow me there

They can weigh me down now

And that is okay

My day in paradise is coming

And I will never feel their weight again

I will sing in paradise an unending song

I will sing with those I know

And with those I never met

We were all saved and now we are one

Singing in paradise

Paradise it may take me a long time to reach you

But this trip is worth the travel

Knowing my burdens cannot follow me there

My feet will walk on streets of gold

I will spread my wings in paradise

I will be draped in all white linen

And I will sing an unending melody

His ears will never get tired of hearing

While I rejoice in paradise

I will be rich for eternity in paradise

I will look back at those I left behind

And I will pray for them like someone prayed for me

At the pearly gates is where I will wait

To guide them into paradise

Sedelia Gardner

Blessing me

You cannot see what lies in my heart

But I can tell you it is something good

Because He keeps on blessing me

I know someone out there prayed for me

Maybe someone I don't even know

Because He keeps on blessing me

He has forgiven me

When others around me have not

And I received another chance

Because He keeps on blessing me

Sedelia Gardner

Flower

A beautiful flower

Growing on sinful soil

The seed is not responsible for the soil

On which it grows on

It is only responsible for growing

Once the water has touched it and the sprout has begun

If the soil is to dry it must still fight to grow

If darkness is blocking the light

Then it must find a way to stretch towards the light

A beautiful flower

Growing on sinful soil

Just another beautiful flower

Growing in His great garden below

Sedelia Gardner

Not Afraid

I am not afraid of tomorrow

Because I have already won my battles against yesterday

And I am the victor of today

I am not afraid of tomorrow

Because my God is my shield and my sword

And the battles we have won together are countless

I am not afraid of tomorrow

Because I serve a God who has no fear

So I will sleep with a smile on my face tonight

Because tomorrow battle is already won

Sedelia Gardner

Myself

*Things are moving a little bit slow and some things are
not moving
At all for me but I will remain patience because your
needs for me
Will last longer in my life than the wants I have for
myself*

*Things are pulling me to the left and some are tugging
me to the
Right but I will remain patience because the path you
have laid out for
Me to travel is better than the one I can pave for myself*

*Things are making me humble and my spirits are high
I want to go out and grab what I think is mine but I
will remain patience the things that you can give me are
more than I can ever give myself*

Sedelia Gardner

Winds of Mercy

Here I stand at the edge of a cliff

And the things in my life have pushed me over the edge

So I fall with my life in Your hands

As I fall I pass people along the way

But I am not afraid to fly

Your wind of mercy glides me through the air

So as I fall I spread my wings

And I let the winds of mercy carry me on

And even thou I fall through the clouds

And I can see the ground below

I am not afraid to fly

Your wind of mercy had been gliding me

Over the grounds below

Ever since I found You

No matter how fast I fall

No matter how close the ground below seems

You are the reason

Why I am not afraid to fly

Sedelia Gardner

Brush my shoulders off

I was kicked down in the dirt

And that is how some of my friends like it

Couldn't keep my head above water

So that gave my family something to talk about

In the mist of it all You found me

So I brush my shoulders off

And I give You the praise

I went down in the waters

So now all the dirt is gone

Friends turned their backs

Because now they have nothing to say

Family has no more gossip to spread

Because it is all washed away

In the mist of it all You lifted me up

So I brush my shoulders off

And I give You the praise

I'm all cleaned up I'm just shinning

You would have never known dirt was even on me

Had I not told you

Even the ones that kicked dirt on me can't believe how clean I am

In the mist of it all You found me

So I brush my shoulders off

And I give You the praise

Sedelia Gardner

Purpose

You woke me up to another day

So I know I woke up with a purpose

My purpose is to talk about You

I can sing stories of praises

Sing of how You brought me from the bottom up

I can leap for joy when I tell them

How You brought me out of the darkness

And into the light

And I can cry an ocean of tears when I talk

About how You saved me

You woke me up to another day

So I know I woke up with a purpose

I know not the stories of the Bible word for word

But I do know the stories of my own life

I know I was blind but now I see

I know I was dead but You rose me from death

I know how You healed the pain in my heart that the doctors couldn't

I know how all I had was a small basket of food and You turned it into

Plenty for my household to eat for unending days

I know how I was lost but You found me

I know the sound of Your voice and the touch of Your hand

I know how You opened up the closed doors

I know how You turned my copper pennies into dollars

I know I woke up this morning with a purpose

And my purpose is to talk about You

Sedelia Gardner

Guide me to the waters

For I have seen the sins of man

Dying for the name of them

Senseless death with a dirty soul

Lord guide me to the waters

A slave can work under the torment of his master

With a smile on his face and tears in his eyes

His death will be a noble one with a clean soul

Because he has been in the waters

Lord guide me to the waters

This pile of dirt was not meant to last forever

But the soul inside was

Let me clean my everlasting soul

Even if I have to walk covered in dirt

Lord guide me to the waters

Sedelia Gardner

Leave my nest

I stood up in my nest

And I looked around to see

What all He had to offer me

It was more than my eyes could see

And it was more than my pockets could hold

I shook off those lose feathers

They were just weighing me down

And I took my first step out

I opened up my winds

But He spread them open for me to fly!

I will take the pain

It is only part of the journey

I will gather up my strength

And put my faith into play

So I can ride the winds

And fly!

Sedelia Gardner

Dance in the Rain

I have to learn to dance in the rain

Even if that means messing up my hair

Hard times require furious acts of dancing

And it is time that I learn

Even if I have to dance alone

I still have to learn some how to dance in the rain

Just let my feet pick up the rhythm of the Sunday morning drum playing

Piano banging and choir singing and get aligned with the pastor preaching

Hard times require furious acts of dancing

And right now hard times are engulfing my soul

So I must learn to dance in the rain

Let the sweat from my brow run down my body

And wash away it all away

I am not worried about a partner

Because this is a dance I must do alone

But I am sure there will be others in the room

Dancing in the rain

Sedelia Gardner

Will I get In

I read about the pearly gates

And the streets all covered in gold

The great land of milk and honey

And a reward of everlasting life

A grand prize for those who followed your rules

I know I have broken a few

And I tried to correct my wrongs

Will your pearly gates open up for me

Lord will I get in

Will I get in

I traveled the road you laid out for me

As best as I could

I didn't always stay on the right path

But Lord I tried

So Lord when you open up the book of life

I hope the good actions outweigh the bad ones

And I hope that it is enough to get me in

Will I get in

I stretched out my hand to those I knew were in need

I even reminded them of Your precious word

I turned the other cheek many times

And sometimes I couldn't

I forgive my enemies in prayer

Just like You said

Will I get in

You made a room for all of Your children

And even placed a chair for them at Your table

Lord I battled through the storms

And the rain

And not once did I forget to give you the praise

And call on Your name

So I am just wondering

When everything is said and done

Will I get in

Sedelia Gardner

Weather

Some feel the rain

And others just get wet

Some just feel a few sprinkles

And others get a down pour

Some get sunny days

And others have days darker than night

Some can keep their head above water

And others just slip and drown

Sedelia Gardner

Anchor

The word is weighing me down it is my anchor

And faith is the chain

I am held in place by my anchor

And the storms can only rattle my chain

The word is down deep in the waters giving strength to my anchor

And each storm is just another link added to my chain

The waters are filled with anchors

And some have broken chains

But I am weighed down by my anchor

And my faith is the chain

Sedelia Gardner

Wrapping Paper

We stand and hold hands and pray

To the very same Father up above

We are all of different colors

But when we pray together

It doesn't matter

But to the outside world it does

We are all a gift to those around us

No matter what color

The wrapping paper is

We each have a different tongue

And many different alters

But one Father

Who treats us all the same

The same blood that protects me

Is the same blood that protects you

And the water cleansed us both

We are all a gift to those around us

No matter what color

The wrapping paper is

The Son saw no color

When He came to die on the cross

To save us all

He made a place in paradise

For me and for you

A mansion filled with many colors

We are all a gift to those around us

No matter what color

The wrapping paper is

Sedelia Gardner

Awaiting

Sometimes I fall

And I can't find the strength to get up again

But He fell

And rose again to carry His cross

To a death that was awaiting Him

Sometimes I cry

And I can't find the strength to stop

But He wept

And wept again as He carried His cross

To a death that was awaiting Him

Sometimes I get lost

And I can't find the strength to get back on my path

But He walked His

And He stayed on His path carrying His cross

To a death that was awaiting Him

Sedelia Gardner

Nail me to the Cross

Nail me to the Cross

I scream

As my enemies hit the spike with the hammer

And pound it into my hand

The things they set up and formed against me

Formed a spike

Nail me to the Cross

I scream

As my enemies pound another spike into my hand

Some of them fall to the ground

But they cannot understand how I still hang high

Nail me to the Cross

I scream

As my enemies pound a spike into my feet

My enemies can only nail me to the Cross

They do not have the strength

To keep me there to die

Sedelia Gardner

Sole

I cannot worry about what type of shoes

That are on my feet

Because I will change them

A 100 times before I get to where I am going

And sometimes it is not what's on your feet

But it is the strength inside

That keeps your feet moving

High heels, wedges, sneakers, flip flops and boots

I have worn them all

And I have yet to find a pair that is strong enough

To last on this journey

Bare feet is what I wore coming into this world

And bare feet is what I will wear when I leave this world

The soles of my feet is what God supplied me with

It is something that will never wear down

Or get out dated

I cannot worry about what type of shoes

That are on my feet

I just have to make sure my soul

Is strong enough to move my sole

That is carrying me on my journey

Sedelia Gardner

Mercy

Lord when you look down from the great heavens

And you find me amongst your children

Have mercy on me

Lord when you look down from the heavenly skies

And you look into my eyes

Remember those are the eyes of a child

Have mercy on me

Lord when you raise the sun

And set the moon in the sky

Remember I lay beneath them both

Have mercy on me

Lord when you open up the store house

And you pour out your many blessings

Have mercy on me

Lord when my end has come

And you open up the book of life

Remember that I tried my best

Have mercy on me

Sedelia Gardner

I Pray to a God

I pray to a God that hear my cries
And even thou my mouth may not speak
My heart does
And He hears my cries

I pray to a forgiving God
And even thou I may not do things that are right
A second chance is given to me
Because He is a forgiving God

I pray to a God that helps me
And even thou I may go down the wrong path
Sometimes
He is still in the mist helping me

I pray to a God that loves me
And even thou the world may turn its back on me
And leave me to die
He will pick me up and carry me on
Because He loves me

Sedelia Gardner

Silent Prayer

I was a child sitting beneath my father's chair
And I could see the tears roll down his cheek
As he looked down at me
With tears I could not understand
There was nothing to be sad about
As far as I could see
But once I had children of my own to protect
I learned what a silent prayer was
His mouth did not speak a word
But his heart was having an intimate conver-
sation with God
A silent prayer
The most powerful prayer a person can give
Many days I seen the tears
Roll down his cheek
As I grew
As I had children of my own
And they grew
His silent prayer kept us safe
And now it is my time to learn the silent prayer
My father has now left me to join our Father
I let the tears roll down my cheek
As my father once did for me
And have my silent intimate conversations with
God
To bless my children with a silent prayer

Sedelia Gardner

68

Author

You wrote a book for me

Many moons ago

Before the world took form my book

Was already on your shelf

You cannot skip ahead and try to read other chapters

No matter what the cards may say

The next page is still a mystery

Those around me can read the pages

Of past chapters that we have written together

My up and downs

My heartache and joy

My tears and my laughter

My darkness and my light

Maybe when they have read my past chapters

Their faith will increase in the author

I know not what the next chapter says

But this book is too good to put down

So I know it will be good because

My God wrote my book

Sedelia Gardner

My Friend Jesus

My friend Jesus is a whisper away
He's worth the songs I sing
And all the praise I give
My friend Jesus will never abandon me
Even when I'm sick, alone and afraid
His soft sweet touch breezes across my cheeks,
The simplest thoughts of him put a smile across my lips,
The purest ideal that is put in my heart is no more than
My friend Jesus the Son of God

Sheri Coleman & Sedelia Gardner

Roll Call "Standing Tall"

Lord I'm here standing tall

Shouting out your name

With no fears at all

Lord I love you like no other

Giving you all the praise and honor

I'm here standing tall

Lord every test I passed

With fears or tears it didn't faze me

I'm still here standing tall

Lord how excellent is your name

I glorify you by standing tall

Lord it's me walking

In the footsteps you ordered

Just for little old me

I'm standing tall,

When everything begin to crumble and fall

I'm still here standing tall

Lord you called me

I'm answering your roll call

Happy to be before you Standing Tall

Sheri Coleman & Sedelia Gardner

Hello Lord I don't know when my day on earth will end or when my final seconds may be up but I will embrace each day as a blessing because it was You that opened up my eyes and gave me a chance to breathe once again. And I will smile when I encounter a task because You know that I am strong enough to handle it. You are my Father and You will never give me more than I can bare. Even thou my shell may look weak on the outside You still saw that I was strong enough on the inside to be one of Your warriors and You blessed me with the gift to live forever for my services. So I will continue to throw up the deuces to the blue skies and continue to sing my songs of praise to you off key. And if the only scripture I can remember on a Sunday morning is "Jesus Wept" I will say it with a strong and loud voice. I know you are the author of my book. You have written my beginning, middle and end. And even thou some chapters look dark you always find a way to put some light in the chapters. But I will continue to give You all the praise the only way I know how through my **Ghetto Love.**

Your Child
Sedelia Gardner

www.ingramcontent.com/pod-product-compliance
Lightning Source LLC
Chambersburg PA
CBHW021207020426
42331CB00003B/250